Colitis Hater's Cookbook

Recipes for Ulcerative Colitis and Crohn's Disease

A Comprehensive Guide to Preparing Recipes During the
Varied Stages of Ulcerative Colitis
and Crohn's Disease

By Jodi Hockinson,
DTR, CDM, CFPP

Colitis Hater's Cookbook
A comprehensive guide to preparing recipes during the varied stages of Ulcerative Colitis and Crohn's Disease

Published by:
Southeast Media Productions
87 Piedmont Dr.
Palm Coast, FL 32164
USA
Phone: 386-503-6832

ISBN-10:1888141611

Please note: The contents of this book are in no way intended for use as a substitute for medical advice. Always consult your physician or dietitian. As every individual case is different, please follow your recommended regimen, including exercise, diet and medications.

The tart cherry juice concentrate used for testing recipes in this cookbook was provided by Traverse Bay Farms, Bellaire, MI, website: TraverseBayFarms.com

Contents

What is IBD?

Inflammatory Bowel Disease (IBD) is a condition which involves the auto-immune system attacking the gastrointestinal system, leading to a number of debilitating symptoms, such as ulcers, diarrhea, severe pain, nausea, fatigue and weight loss as well as rectal and intestinal bleeding.

The two most common forms of IBD are ulcerative colitis and Crohn's disease. Crohn's disease can manifest itself in any area(s) of the gastrointestinal system from the mouth to the anus. Ulcerative colitis is found only in the colon and/or rectum.

Up to 80% of Crohn's patients ultimately require surgery. About one third of ulcerative colitis patients end up needing surgery. Virtually all Crohn's and ulcerative colitis sufferers require continuous medication, even during remission, as a lifelong treatment.

IBD is not contagious, and although there can be a genetic predisposition, it is not likely that you will pass the disease on to your children.

Diagnosing Crohn's or ulcerative colitis can be difficult, as there are a number of illnesses that exhibit similar symptoms, such as pancreatitis, hemorrhoids, colon cancer or even gallbladder disease. In fact, Crohn's can appear in the colon, just as ulcerative colitis, but with some significant differences. Ulcerative colitis occurs in the lining of the colon and rectum, whereas Crohn's affects the entire wall of the intestine, resulting in abscesses and fistulas (tunnels in the intestinal wall).

The granuloma cell can appear (biopsy) in Crohn's, but not in ulcerative colitis. In addition, blood tests with positive results for ANCA (antineutrophil cytoplasmic antibody) can indicate the presence of ulcerative colitis, whereas positive results for ASCA (anti-Saccharomyces cerevisiae antibody) can indicate the presence of Crohn's.

The symptoms for both Crohn's and ulcerative colitis can be quite similar, although there are differences between the two. For example, ulcers in ulcerative colitis are more superficial, whereas Crohn's ulcers tend to be deeper.

There is generally more bleeding with ulcerative colitis than with Crohn's. There is more likelihood of bowel obstructions with Crohn's, due to possible strictures (narrowing).

Although diet is not believed to be a cause of IBD, it can absolutely affect symptoms, even during remission. For example, caffeine can induce, or exacerbate, diarrhea.

Hard to digest foods, such as fried foods or raw vege-tables, or even seeds, could contribute to bowel obstruction or intestinal discomfort.

Symptoms and flare-ups can also be attributed to psychological pressure, such as stressful situations, and psychological conditions, such as depression, which can influence intestinal function.

Nutrition can be a major issue with a vicious cycle, especially when one of the symptoms of IBD is malabsorption, which can cause anemia and/or vitamin deficiency.

The malabsorption itself can lead to fatigue and weight loss as well as diarrhea, and eventually even osteoporosis.

Malabsorption (due to reduced efficiency of the small intestine) is more common in Crohn's; malnourishment (due to diarrhea or insufficient food intake) is more common in ulcerative colitis. Malnourishment is also a product of malabsorption.

Iron and magnesium deficiency are common in IBD sufferers. It is possible that your physician will test your blood routinely for deficiencies in B_{12}, vitamin D, folic acid, zinc, iron and calcium.

These vitamins and minerals can be supplemented by multi-vitamins, except in some cases in which there is no possible absorption of B_{12}, which would require periodical injections or nasal gel.

Nutrition and Vitamins

Eating with a restricted diet is much more likely to result in vitamin deficiency. To make matters worse, malabsorption and malnutrition are both products of IBD. That being said, one of the most important things to remember when eating with IBD is that foods which are easier to digest will be easier on your intestines, giving your system a chance to rest and heal. Therefore, vitamins should be supplemented. Keeping a food diary can be enormously helpful in determining what foods and dieting habits work best in each individual. In fact, a specific diet that works for one person may not work for another.

To go easier on your digestive tract, small meals that are eaten frequently are much gentler on your system than larger, less frequent meals. Fish is easier to digest than chicken, pork or beef.

Foods that are less fibrous are more easily tolerated, and less likely to cause obstructions. Therefore, breaking down the fiber in your foods can help tremendously. Broken down fiber can be accomplished in some foods by freezing before cooking, and boiling, baking or steaming until soft. One difficult idea is the thought of canned foods, which, in the canning process, have lost many nutrients. However, in many instances, canned foods can be much less fibrous than their fresh counterparts, even when cooked. To make matters worse, medications can strip minerals and vitamins from your system, as well.

Although the above processes may strip many nutrients from the foods we consume, sometimes the higher priority becomes giving the intestines a rest, and supplementing with multivitamins. Many publications recommend a normal multivitamin, with iron, calcium and vitamin D. Multivitamins can be purchased in liquid form as well as pills. Liquid form may be better tolerated, especially during Phase One (initial onset or flare) of your condition. In some cases, vitamin B_{12} can no longer be absorbed, especially in the case of some intestinal damage or removal. In these cases, Vitamin B_{12} must be injected regularly.

Malabsorption can already be causing deficiencies in the following areas:
- Calcium and Vitamin D – supplementing can help lower the risk for osteoporosis.
- Iron – supplementing can help increase immunity, fighting anemia, fatigue and infection.
- Zinc – supplementing can help fighting reduced immunity, loss of appetite and skin changes.
- Vitamin B_{12} – supplementing, either orally or by injection, if needed, helps in the manufacture of red blood cells, helps fight against nerve damage, anemia, fatigue, and sensitive skin.

- Vitamin A – supplementing can help vision (including night blindness), immunity and skin.
- Vitamin E - supplementing can help with fat absorption and help lower the risk for heart disease and stroke.
- Vitamin K – supplementing helps in blood coagulation and manufacture of body proteins in the blood, bones and kidneys.

Blood loss and diarrhea can cause deficiencies in
- Magnesium – supplementing can help maintain body cells in muscles and nerves, fighting against nausea, weakness and irregular heartbeat.
- Iron – supplementing can help increase immunity, fighting anemia, fatigue and infection.

If you are lactose intolerant, and cannot consume milk or dairy products, you should be sure to supplement with calcium and vitamin D to lower your risk for osteoporosis.

Contraindications:

Be aware of contraindications among your medications. Carefully read the warnings and information offered with all of your medications, and be sure that every prescribing physician is fully aware of all medications that you are taking.

In addition, there are certain foods or supplements that can affect the behavior of your medications, or exacerbate your condition. For example, garlic supplements may thin your blood, which is the last thing you want when you are bleeding, such as during a flare of ulcerative colitis. The effects of some antibiotics can be reduced by simultaneous consumption of calcium, and one type of penicillin can be destroyed when consumed at the same time with citrus fruits or juice.

Do's and Don'ts During the Three Phases

It may be easiest to begin with a list of foods to try avoiding, then working from the beginning on three phases of your condition. At the onset of your new diet, and especially during a flare, it will be important to be aware of foods and ingredients that can exacerbate inflammation, contribute to obstruction or cause general intestinal discomfort. Following is a list of foods that can help meet the above criteria.

Phase One

Phase 1 involves the time just after the flare-up, or the initial diagnosis period. During this phase, you may have experienced a flare so severe that your body required parenteral nutrition (intravenous feeding), and you will need to very carefully watch everything you ingest. This is an ideal time to begin your food diary. The more information you record, the more likely you will be able to recognize patterns that will emerge.

During Phase One, your physician or dietitian will give you a specific diet, which may involve liquid nourishment such as Ensure, protein shakes and very soft foods, e.g., applesauce and mashed potatoes.

During this first phase, food should be soft enough to cut with a fork, low residue, and should not require much chewing. The idea at this point is to give your bowels a chance to rest.

You will begin with a small list of easily digestible foods, gradually, and carefully adding more items to your list. Continually record each meal in a food diary (see Food Diary section), along with any symptoms, etc. Keep track of foods eaten, when you rest, even when you go to sleep and wake up.

Care should be taken to eat small, frequent meals rather than larger meals, to help ease the strain on the digestive system. For example, instead of three standard meals a day, try three very small meals, with small snacks between each and at bed time.

Fiber (especially insoluble fiber) should be avoided as much as possible - for example, by cooking foods until soft, perhaps even freezing before cooking, as the freezing process works to help break down the fiber in foods.

You will want to keep to a low-residue diet (reducing the amount of fiber and foods difficult to digest) at this point, especially when you first get out of the hospital.

Be sure that the foods you eat are easy to digest. For example, fried foods take much longer to digest than foods that are steamed, boiled or baked. Don't saute in oil – use water, cooking until all water is reduced. Remember, fish is much easier to digest than chicken or beef.

Fiber should be broken down as much as possible. For example, instead of fresh, peeled apples, try applesauce or peeled apples that are baked, steamed or boiled until soft.

Avoid peelings, skins, and seeds. Be wary of fruits and vegetables with skins or seeds that cannot be removed, such as strawberries and raspberries. Also, be cautious of foods that cause gas. Anything that can cause normal intestinal discomfort can be a source of much worse effects when inflammation is already an issue.

Avoid insoluble fibers, such as apple peels, grape skins, whole grain wheat and whole bran products. Indeed, there are a great number of healthy foods that can contribute to inflammation or obstruction, and should be avoided.

Avoid ingredients, such as caffeine, that can cause stimulation of bowel movements. Again, try to eat only foods that are easy to digest, only gradually and cautiously adding new items to your diet as you begin to heal.

Beware intolerance to fructose or lactose. For example, lactose intolerance can occur during intestinal inflammation, or when there is damage to the small intestinal lining. This can result in cramping, diarrhea and bloating, which can exacerbate your condition.

In cases of lactose intolerance, milk can be substituted with calcium-fortified soy, almond, rice milk or Lactaid. Some types of yogurt may also be tolerated more than others, such as Lactaid brand yogurt, as they contain bacteria that actually break down lactose during incubation.

In addition, milk can be treated with lactase drops, which can be purchased, if not locally, from a number of online sources such as Amazon.com. Lactase pills are also available to be taken in conjunction with milk ingestion.

When checking ingredients for products containing lactose, watch for ingredients such as lactose, milk, whey, curds, dry milk solids, milk by-products or milk powder.

Dairy products highest in lactose include milk and ice cream; dairy products with some lactose include yogurt, cottage cheese and sherbet; dairy products with the least amount of lactose include butter, sour cream, half & half, blue cheese, American cheese and Swiss cheese.

In many cases of lactose intolerance, milk can be substituted with calcium-fortified soy, almond, rice milk or Lactaid. Some types of yogurt may also be tolerated more than others, as they contain bacteria that actually break down lactose during incubation.

In addition, milk can be treated with lactase drops, which can be purchased, if not locally, from a number of online sources such as Amazon.com. Lactase pills are also available to be taken in conjunction with milk ingestion.

Products available with the Lactaid brand name include milk, yogurt, cottage cheese and ice cream.

There are also cheeses available on the market that advertise lactose free products, such as Finlandia cheeses, which include imported Swiss, Muenster, Havarti and Gouda.

Foods and Ingredients to Avoid
Or to Approach with Extreme Caution:

Alcohol of any type (e.g., beer wine or liquor)

Legumes, such as beans, peas, lentils

Soy oil, safflower oil, corn oil, cottonseed oil,

sunflower oil, peanut oil, saturated fat, animal fat

Seeds

Dried or raw fruits, nuts (except small amounts of smooth nut butter, such as almond or cashew butter) Any outside skin of fruit, such as the skin of cherries, grapes, apples, pears, peaches

Fruits with seeds or skins that cannot be removed, such as blackberries, blueberries, cranberries, grapes, kiwi, orange (due to membranes) pomegranates, prunes, currants, dates, figs, grapefruit, raisins, raspberries, strawberries, tangerines, dried fruits, grapes (unless peeled)

Breads and flour with whole wheat, seeded rye, whole grains, any w/seeds, nuts or bran, soybean meal (raw soy meal)

Whole grain, brown or wild rice

High fiber cereals, such as Wheaties, All Bran, Bran Flakes, Shredded Wheat, Fiber One, Raisin Bran, Great Grains, Granola or Grape Nuts, All Bran, Oat Bran, Corn Bran, Corn cereals, Fiber One, and any with dried fruit/nuts

Whole wheat pasta

Whole grain wheat crackers, such as Trisket, multigrain, any with seeds, cracked wheat, corn tortillas, corn meal

Raw vegetables

Vegetables that cause gas, or with seeds or insoluble fiber such as skins that cannot be removed, such as beans, all varieties of legumes (except smooth peanut butter), celery, broccoli (unless cooked until very soft), Brussels sprouts, cauliflower, cabbage, alfalfa sprouts, bamboo shoots, eggplant, kohlrabi, radishes, turnips, beet juice, beets or beet greens, corn and popcorn, cucumbers, garlic & onion (garlic and onion can be used for flavor, but should be removed before serving), peppers, sauerkraut, zucchini

Organ meats, processed meats, sandwich spreads from meat, sausages, bacon

Chicken or turkey - dark meat and skin-remove before cooking, not afterwards.

Any meat that is fatty, tough or chewy – this will be more difficult to digest; any meat with skin

Caution seafood: abalone, clam, conch, crab, lobster, mussel, octopus, oysters, shrimp, squid

Sugar alcohols such as mannitol, xylitol or sorbitol

Chocolate of any type

Carbonated beverages

Sulfites

All fried foods and fast foods

Honey – at least at first – it has been known to cause botulism in infants.

MSG and artificial sweeteners

Corn syrup, anything above 6g sugar per serving-such as some sweet cereals or desserts

Caffeine, tea, coffee and decaf coffee (these can act as stimulants which can induce bowel movement)

Beverages and foods that are ice cold or extremely hot

Foods to Begin Trying During Phase One:

Egg whites, limit yolks to one per day (use pre-pasteurized eggs, egg substitute or dried egg whites)

Strained fruit juices (with no pulp or sediment), such as apple, cherry, grape, cranberry, calcium fortified orange juice (low acid, no pulp) - all diluted with equal parts of water. Too much of any fruit juice can cause intestinal discomfort or diarrhea.

Protein shakes (not high fiber), drinks that are glucose and electrolyte based, such as Gatorade, diluted with water

Broth - meat, poultry, fish or vegetable

Tilapia, salmon, cod, halibut, grouper, flounder, whitefish (no skin or bones)

Nut butter, smooth only, small quantities- such as cashew or almond butter

Soy milk, tofu, soy cheeses (preferably all calcium enriched)

Milk and milk products, if you are not lactose intolerant, low fat or fat free

Bananas (small amounts)

Canned varieties of peaches (not halves), apricots, grapefruit, pineapple, mandarin orange sections

Cantaloupe, watermelon (seedless) and honeydew melon

Cream of wheat, cream of rice, barley and oatmeal, but only if cooked until very soft

Mushrooms, well cooked

Any white flour cracker with no added fiber/bran, whole grains or seeds- for example, oyster crackers, table water crackers, saltine crackers

White bread, white rice, Flour tortillas (very small

amounts), white pasta

Leafy greens like spinach and collards, cooked until soft

Vegetables that have no peel or seeds, cooked until soft, such as carrots and potatoes (both peeled and well cooked)
Squash, such as acorn, spaghetti and butternut, cooked until soft

Sugar (keep under 6g per serving)

Pudding made with skim milk, soy milk or lactose free milk

Cinnamon

Jelly, used in very small amounts, clear - no seeds, no fruit pieces

Salt and pepper - small amounts

Phase Two

Once you can see yourself recovering from the severe phase of inflammation, you have entered the second phase. You will begin adding foods to your diet, but slowly and with caution.

This is another crucial stage in keeping a food diary. For example, tomatoes, tomato sauce and tomato paste may each be tolerated differently. Any items that seem to aggravate your condition can be crossed off, for the time being, at least, to be pensively tried at a later date.

When running across recipes that contain questionable ingredients, use a substitute that you are more comfortable with, or leave out the ingredient entirely if it will not affect the finished product. Otherwise, find a different recipe, or prepare a different dish. Keep a recipe box with converted recipes that work!

Foods include everything in the Phase One list, plus:

Increased amounts of foods that will work to solidify bowel movements, such as rice, bananas and white bread. Cheese will also help, but be wary of lactose intolerance.

Begin to add more soluble fibers, albeit with care, such as oats and finely milled grains, such as white flour, soluble fiber products, such as Metamucil (Only with physician or dietitian recommendation. Products such as this work to actually help bind stool together, but used too soon can exacerbate your condition).

Canned (or cooked until soft) green beans, asparagus, skinless and seedless tomatoes, tomato sauce or paste

Chopped cucumber without skin and without seeds

Peeled cherries and grapes

Ground beef, very low fat, small amounts only, pork tenderloin, or lean beef, cooked until tender

Chicken or turkey meat, white skinless only, cooked until tender

Oil and vinegar dressing, made with canola or olive oil

Lettuce – head, Boston or Bibb; arugula, endive and kale

Peppers – roasted and skinned

Cauliflower – cooked until soft

Parsnips, sweet potatoes, yams (all peeled and cooked until soft)

Pumpkin (cooked until soft)

Phase Three

At this point, you have essentially recovered from the flare and are returning to normal activities. This is again a good time to continue with your food diary, to help recognize foods as well as other outside influences, such as resting habits (or lack thereof) and certain stressful situations, that may contribute to intestinal discomfort.

Maintenance medications are typically taken, even once you are in remission, and you may be able to return to an unrestricted food intake regimen. However, it may be prudent to continue with a diet that is less likely to play any part in a resulting flare.

By now, you probably have a basic idea of patterns that have emerged in your food diary. Again, it is important to maintain your food diary, as the same food that did not aggravate your system in the past may aggravate it in the future, especially if consumed in a different quantity, or when combined with another food.

Foods that did not work in the beginning may be pensively added to your diet. Be sure to accurately record what is consumed, when, how much, and whether you experience discomfort.

The diet that has been kept to three small meals per day, with small snacks between, should have become a habit at this point, and should be continued.

Keeping a Food Diary

Conflicting information seems to run rampant when it comes to diet for IBD sufferers. One publication will state a certain food is OK for digestion, while another will swear against it.

For example, there seems to be a difference of opinion concerning dairy products and lactose intolerance. One publication will state that lactose intolerance is not widespread among IBD sufferers, while another will warn that intolerance is more likely, due to inflammation.

The problem is that every case is different. Everyone must have a starting point, and everyone must learn to read messages from his (or her) own intestines.

Between all of the publications concerning IBD, there does seem to be one common matter of great importance: keep a food diary. When your physician or dietitian gives you a regimen, keep as close as you can to following every bit of advice – it could mean the difference in avoiding, or causing, a major flare up!

Keep a food diary that is concise, but complete. Charts with categories work well for comparing and discovering patterns. It is vital to remember that a food tolerated once does not mean that it will be a food always tolerated. Foods in certain portions can be different than the same foods in larger, or smaller, portions.

Study your diary for patterns. Without your diary, there are patterns you may never have realized, such as different sources of stress, combinations of foods, or even the time of day a certain food is consumed. Every detail can make a difference.

Committing yourself to constantly entering information can be tough, but rewarding. In addition, there is a positive result that comes with keeping track of what you do. Once you recognize certain repeated behaviors, you can begin to develop habits that will promote continued healing.

Keep your diary organized with as many information entries, albeit concise, as possible. For example, you can look back and see how many meals you had in one day, how large they were, whether you were experiencing stress, and what types of discomfort, pain or other symptoms that you experienced.

Following is an example of a table with a few entries:

SAMPLE FOOD DIARY CHART

Time of Day	Ate & how much	Drank & how much	Rest afterwards?	Family stress?	Work stress?	Cigarette?	Symptoms?
9:00wake up							
9:15	One egg, scrambled, ½ piece toast with ½ teaspoon grape jelly	⅓ cup apple juice	Yes-15 minutes	No	Yes – project presentation at 10:00	Yes, during rest	15 minutes After breakfast, loose stool

Additional Notes

To keep hydrated, especially during episodes involving diarrhea, drink lots of water, at least 8-10 8-oz. glasses per day. Loose stool is often experienced during inflammation in the colon, which reduces its ability to absorb water. Avoid drinking iced cold beverages, as these can cause cramping and diarrhea.

Remember, keep portions and servings small, and always record the time and amount consumed. A smaller amount of one food may be tolerated more easily than an increased portion of the same food. Instead of three meals a day, have three very small meals, with snacks between each meal.

Don't sauté or fry foods. Instead of sautéing, use water with a nonstick pan, such as Teflon or Thermalon coated pans, for cooking.

If a small amount of oil is needed for cooking (such as a recipe that calls for a "greased" baking dish), try using a lightly sprayed mist of canola or olive oil.

Pump spray bottles can be purchased at gourmet stores or local department stores, which can be used with canola or olive oil, instead of commercial cooking spray with additives.

Flax oil is good for digestion, but not if heated – heating flax oil compromises the good qualities of the oil.

When cooking with onions or garlic for flavor, always remove before serving. The flavor is OK, the onion or garlic itself is not, as it will produce gas, causing intestinal discomfort.

Avoid raw eggs; use pre-pasteurized eggs, egg white powder (plus water – follow package instructions) or egg substitute.

Canned foods are not as nutritious, but they typically contain fiber that is much more broken down than their fresh or cooked counterparts. It is important to help supplement the nutritional shortages with vitamin supplements and products that are vitamin enriched, such as calcium fortified orange juice.

Eat lots of fish! The omega-3 fatty acids found in the oils of shrimp, fish and other seafood help suppress inflammation. Fish can be tolerated much better than chicken or beef, and can be eaten often.

Seafood high in Omega 3 includes anchovy, trout, herring, mackerel and mullet. Seafood moderately high in Omega 3 includes tuna, whitefish, smelt, carp and sturgeon.

A pressure cooker can be used to break down fibers in foods when cooking. Tender foods, especially just after a flare-up, are much better tolerated.

Check labels for added ingredients, such as msg and sulfites. Generic brands often contain fewer additives than their name brand counterparts.

Always cook vegetables well, never consuming raw vegetables except lettuce, and peeling whenever appropriate, such as carrots and potatoes. Never eat skins, such as on squash or pumpkin.

An ideal diet might be vegetarian, with eggs, milk and fish allowed. However, some recipes with chicken and beef have been included, as your system may be able to tolerate them. If you are going to eat chicken or beef, do everything you can to break down the fiber and help make it easier on your system before consuming it.

When cooking any type of meat, be sure it is completely cooked.

Canned can be better, especially at first – not quite as nutritious, but fiber will be broken down better, and nutrition needs should be made up with supplements.

Last, and by all means not least, this book is not intended as a substitute for medical advice, and every case is different. Therefore, it is vital that you follow the recommended diet and exercise regimen prescribed by your physician or dietitian!

Phase One Recipes

Chamomile Tea

1 chamomile tea bag
1 cup water
lemon juice

Pour boiling water over tea bags. Steep for at least 10 minutes. Add lemon to taste and enjoy.

Mango Shake

1 ripe mango, peeled, pitted and chopped
1 cup vanilla yogurt
(see pp 13-14 about lactose)
1½ cups milk
(see pp 13-14 about lactose)

¼ cup sugar

Combine in blender. Mix until smooth. Makes about 3 ½ cups.

Orange Shake

1 cup milk
(see pp 13-14 about lactose)
1 cup low acid, pulp free orange juice
½ cup sugar
1 teaspoon vanilla extract

Combine ingredients in blender.   Blend about 30 seconds and serve.

Vanilla Shake

1 cup milk
(see pp 13-14 about lactose)
1 cup yogurt
(see pp 13-14 about lactose)
¼ teaspoon vanilla
⅛ cup to ¼ cup sugar, to taste

Combine ingredients in an electric blender.   Blend until smooth. Serves 2.

Cranberry Tea

1 cup water
1 cup cranberry juice

Stir ingredients together. Serve warm. Serves 2.

Apple Pancakes

1 apple
1 teaspoon lemon juice
2 tablespoons brown sugar
⅛ teaspoon cinnamon
Batter from one recipe of pancakes

Peel, core and finely chop apple. Combine with lemon juice, sugar and cinnamon. Cook in a small saucepan, stirring often, for 3-4 minutes, or until liquid is reduced and apples are soft.

Remove from heat and set aside. Allow to cool for at least 5 minutes. While apples are cooling, prepare pancake batter.

Fold in apples, and cook as directed in pancake recipe. Serve lightly sprinkled with powdered sugar. Makes about 1 dozen.

Pancakes

2 eggs
3 tablespoons canola oil
1 cup skim milk
(see pp 13-14 about lactose)
¾ teaspoon salt
1¾ teaspoons baking powder
1¼ to 1¾ cups white flour (less for thinner pancakes,
more for thicker pancakes)

Separate eggs. Discard one yolk and place remaining yolk in a large mixing bowl. Set aside. Beat whites with an electric mixer until stiff. Set aside.

Add remaining ingredients to yolk and blend with electric mixer until smooth. Fold in egg whites. Lightly coat skillet with canola oil.

Pour, in 4-inch circles, into a preheated non-stick skillet (Thermalon coating recommended).

Cook until the surface of each pancake begins to bubble and become slightly dry. Gently lift the pancake with a spatula to check the doneness on the bottom.

Once the bottom lightly browns, then flip over and cook until lightly browned. Makes 10-12 pancakes.

Potato Pancakes

1 cup mashed potatoes (see recipe)
¾ cup white flour
¼ cup milk
(see pp 13-14 about lactose)
¼ teaspoon onion powder
¼ teaspoon salt
1 egg
½ teaspoon canola oil

Combine ingredients, except canola oil, in mixing bowl. Blend well with electric mixer.

Preheat a nonstick skillet over medium heat. Add canola oil, spreading thinly with spatula.

Add pancake batter in spooned dollops (about 2 tablespoons each).

Lifting up edge each half minute to check for doneness, flip when slightly browned.

Cook until flip side is browned, check for doneness on the inside, and serve. Makes about 1 dozen.

Boiled Eggs

1 to 6 eggs
water and ice

Place egg(s) in saucepan. Cover with cold water. Bring to a boil. Boil for 10 minutes. Drain. "Shock" the eggs by soaking immediately in ice water – about two cups water, 1 cup ice.

Allow eggs to cool in ice water – at least 5 minutes (Shocking the eggs will cause the shell to peel off more easily). The eggs are now ready for use or may be returned to fridge for later use.

Scrambled Eggs

2 eggs, one yolk removed
(pre-pasteurized)
1 ounce skim milk
(see pp 13-14 about lactose)

Blend eggs and milk with a whisk in a small mixing bowl. Cook in a non-stick skillet, stirring constantly, until desired level of doneness is reached. Serves one.

French Toast

½ cup milk
(see pp 13-14 about lactose)
2 eggs, one yolk removed
(pre-pasteurized)
6-8 slices white bread
½ teaspoon canola oil

Combine milk and eggs in a large mixing bowl. Blend with a whisk until smooth.

Preheat a large nonstick skillet over medium-high heat. Drop in canola oil, spreading well with spatula.

Dip one slice of bread into egg mixture. Flip over, making sure both sides are covered in mixture. Place bread in heated skillet.

Set aside remaining bread. Wait to dip each bread slice into egg mixture until just before placing into skillet.

Depending on the size of the skillet, dip more bread slices into egg mixture and place into skillet as room allows.

Cook soaked bread in skillet until browned on both sides. Serve topped lightly with powdered sugar. Makes 6-8 pieces.

Poached Eggs

eggs (pre-pasteurized)
water
1 tablespoon vinegar (optional)

Fill saucepan with at least 3" water. Bring to boil, reduce heat and simmer. Add vinegar. This will help the egg stay together. Gently drop in each egg (it can be easier to break each egg into a small dish then easing it into the water). Swirl water with a spoon – this will also help the egg to stay together and retain a nice shape. Cook for about 3 minutes, or until desired doneness is reached. Remove with slotted spoon. Allow excess water to drip into saucepan for about 10 seconds before plating.

Applesauce

10 apples
½ cup brown sugar
½ teaspoon lemon juice

Peel and core apples. Chop coarsely. Combine all in crockpot; cook for 7-8 hours on low or 4-5 hours on high. Blend with potato masher. Stir well. Serve warm or chilled. Makes 2-3 cups.

Vanilla Yogurt

¾ cup skim milk
(see pp 13-14 about lactose)
2 teaspoons white flour
1½ teaspoons vanilla extract
2 tablespoons sugar
2 cups plain nonfat yogurt
(see pp 13-14 about lactose)

Combine all ingredients, except yogurt, in a medium saucepan. Stir with a whisk until smooth.

Cook over medium high heat, stirring frequently, for about 10 minutes.

Remove from from heat. Chill, then stir into yogurt. Serves 2-3.

Broiled Grouper

2 grouper filets, ½ to ¾" thick
olive oil
lemon juice

Lightly coat a cooking pan with olive oil. Brush filets, first with lemon juice, then with olive oil.

Broil about 4 minutes per side or until meat flakes off with a fork. Serves 2.

Homemade Low-fat Yogurt

1 quart low fat milk
(see pp 13-14 about lactose)

5 g yogurt culture (or as per package instructions) or
3 tablespoons of prepared yogurt

Heat milk to boiling point, then allow to cool to lukewarm, about 110° F.

Combine ½ cup of milk with yogurt culture, blending until culture has dissolved. Incubate in yogurt maker for 4-5 hours, or until desired consistency is reached. Refrigerate to halt the incubation process.

Baked Flounder

2 flounder filets ½- ¾" thick
2 tablespoons Olive oil
2 tablespoons lemon juice
Salt and pepper

Lightly coat a baking pan with olive oil. Preheat oven to 450° F. Rinse and pat dry the flounder filets. Combine the olive oil and lemon juice. Brush filets with olive oil mixture.

Lightly sprinkle with salt and pepper. Bake 5-6 minutes or until fish flakes with a fork. Serves 2.

Smoked Salmon Pâté

½ pound smoked salmon
1 tablespoon lemon juice
½ package cream cheese   (4 oz)

Blend with electric mixer until smooth, about 2-3 minutes. Serve over crackers. Makes about 1 cup.

Marinated Grilled Fish

two fish filets, ½ to ¾" thick
½ cup olive oil
⅛ cup lemon juice
⅛ teaspoon onion powder
⅛ teaspoon garlic powder

Blend ingredients well in a small mixing bowl. Set aside ⅛ cup. Add fish, coating well. Soak in refrigerator 30 minutes.

In a 450° F preheated oven, Bake for 8-10 minutes or until fish flakes off with fork. Brush lightly with remaining marinade before serving. Serves 2.

Variation: brush both sides of fish with marinade, cook for 5-6 minutes or until fish flakes off with fork. Serves 2.

Steamed Cod

2 cod filets, 3-4 ounces each

Place filets in steamer. Steam for 12-14 minutes or until fish flakes with a fork. To serve, Drizzle with melted margarine or olive oil. Serves 2.

Variation: Add a drizzle of lemon juice.

Egg Drop Soup

2 cups vegetable or chicken broth
1 egg

Bring broth to a boil. While heating, stir egg well, with a fork or whisk, in a small mixing bowl.

Once broth has reached a boil, stir soup as quickly as possible while adding egg. Boil an additional minute until all egg is cooked. Serves 2.

Egg Salad

⅓ cup mayonnaise
3 boiled eggs, 2 yolks discarded, finely chopped

Blend well in medium mixing bowl. Serves 2-3.

Devilled Eggs

one dozen eggs
⅓ cup mayonnaise
¼ tsp salt

Boil eggs (see boiled eggs recipe). Peel. Cut 6 eggs in half and discard yolks. Coarsely chop remaining eggs and place in food processor or blender with mayonnaise, and salt.

Blend until smooth. Pipe into the 12 egg white halves. Chill. Makes one dozen.

Boiled Potatoes

2 large potatoes
2 quarts water

Peel and chop potatoes. Cover with water in a medium saucepan. Heat to boiling. Boil 25-30 minutes or until potatoes are soft.

Drain and serve. Serving suggestions: Drizzle with olive oil, or top with mushroom or Alfredo sauce. Serves 4.

Mashed Potatoes

2 large potatoes
¼ cup skim milk
(see pp 13-14 about lactose)

2 tablespoons margarine or butter

Peel and cut potatoes into chunks. Boil in salted water until soft. Drain.

Mash with potato masher, then add milk and margarine, continuing to mash until smooth. Makes 4 servings..

Cooked Mushrooms

1 pound mushrooms
water

Cover mushrooms with water in a medium saucepan. Boil until tender.

Variation: To steam, place in steamer for 25 minutes.

Egg Sauce

1 cup skim milk
(see pp 13-14 about lactose)
2 tablespoons white flour
2 hard boiled eggs, one yolk discarded
½ teaspoon salt

Combine milk with flour and salt in a small mixing bowl. Blend with whisk or fork until smooth. Add yolk and blend thoroughly. Place in saucepan.

Chop egg whites and add to saucepan. Heat, stirring frequently, to boiling. Reduce heat and simmer one minute. Serve over fish, bread or vegetables.

Mayonnaise

1 cup canola oil
2 egg whites (pre-pasteurized),
or egg white powder (plus water) equivalent
¼ teaspoon ground mustard
½ teaspoon salt
2 teaspoons sugar
3 teaspoons lemon juice

Place egg whites in a medium to large mixing bowl. Blend with an electric mixer until stiff, but not dry.

Very gradually drizzle in ¾ cup of canola oil while blending.

Gradually blend remaining ingredients, then remainder of canola oil last. Keep refrigerated in an airtight container. Keeps for 2-3 days. Makes about 2 cups.

Vanilla Pudding

3 tablespoons white flour
½ cup sugar
2 cups skim milk
(see pp 13-14 about lactose)

2 eggs, one yolk discarded
1 teaspoon vanilla extract

Blend all ingredients with a whisk until smooth. Cook in a non-stick saucepan over medium to high heat, stirring frequently, until mixture begins to thicken, about 20 minutes.

Remove from heat, pour into serving dishes and allow to cool. Pudding will thicken more as it cools. Serve warm or chilled. Serves 4.

*Watch for lactose intolerance. This can be substituted with Lactaid, soy milk or almond milk.

Phase Two Recipes

Peach Shake

1 fresh peach, pit removed, peeled and quartered
(steamed until soft),
or ½ cup frozen peaches (steamed until soft)
or ½ of a 15 ounce can peeled peaches
in peach juice (drained)
½ cup skim milk
(see pp 13-14 about lactose)
¾ cup non-fat yogurt
(see pp 13-14 about lactose)
1 tablespoon sugar

Combine peach and milk in a blender. Blend until smooth. Gradually add in yogurt and sugar. Makes about 2¼ cups.

Apple Crepes

½ cup white flour
¾ cup skim milk*
1 egg
(See Additional Notes section concerning raw eggs)
one recipe cooked apples

Crepes: in a medium bowl, combine flour, milk and egg. Blend with an electric mixer until smooth.

Preheat a 9-inch non-stick skillet on high for about 30 seconds. Lightly spray canola oil onto the heated surface. Quickly place 2½ tablespoons of batter into pan. Lift the skillet and tilt, rotating the angle of the tilt until the bottom surface of skillet is covered with the batter.

Reduce heat to medium/medium high. Cook for about 30-60 seconds, until the bottom surface of the crepe becomes lightly browned and the exposed surface, although moist, will lose its wet-batter look.

Do not flip over. To remove from skillet, turn skillet upside down over serving dish and allow the crepe to fall out on its own.

Proceed to cook crepes in the same fashion until batter is gone. Makes 6-8 crepes. Spoon a portion of cooked apples towards the one edge of a crepe, roll and serve. Top rolled crepes with any remaining cooked apples. Makes 6-8.

Cherry Yogurt Crepes

One recipe Apple Crepes (less apples)
one recipe cherry sauce
1 cup vanilla yogurt
(see pp 13-14 about lactose)

Follow directions for making crepes. Blend yogurt with ¾ of cherry sauce. Use for crepe filling.

Drizzle crepes with remaining sauce. Makes 4-6.

Peach Yogurt

1 fresh peach, pit removed, peeled and quartered
and steamed until soft,
or ½ cup frozen peaches (steamed until soft),
or ½ of a 15 ounce can peeled peaches
in peach juice (drained)
2 tablespoons sugar
1 cup plain yogurt
(see pp 13-14 about lactose)

Add sugar to peaches, stirring until sugar is completely dissolved. Chill. Gently fold into yogurt. Serves 2.

Cherry Vanilla Yogurt

1 tablespoon tart cherry juice concentrate
1 cup vanilla yogurt
(see pp 13-14 about lactose)
2 tablespoons powdered sugar

Stir cherry concentrate and sugar until sugar is
dissolved. Combine with yogurt. Stir until well
blended. Serves 2.

Creamed Rice

¾ cup skim milk*
1 tablespoon white flour
1½ cups cooked white rice

Combine milk and flour in a small mixing bowl. Stir
with a fork or whisk until smooth. Place in a medium
saucepan together with rice. Cook over medium-high
heat, stirring frequently, until thickened.

Serving suggestion: serve topped with a drizzle of
cherry sauce or a dab of seedless jam.

Salmon Croquettes

¼ pound cooked salmon,
or one 5 oz. can skinless boneless salmon
1 egg
¾ cup Italian bread crumbs
½ cup milk
(see pp 13-14 about lactose)
one recipe for egg sauce

Lightly coat a cookie sheet with canola oil. Preheat oven to 350° F.

Combine ingredients, except for egg sauce, in a mixing bowl. Blend until all is evenly distributed.

With wet hands, separate into 12 equal portions. Shape each portion into a ball, pat to ½ thickness.

Place on cookie sheet Bake at 350° F for 20-25 minutes or until cooked through. While croquettes are cooking, prepare egg sauce.

Serve croquettes topped with egg sauce. Serves 4.

Stuffed Cod in Pouches

4 cod filets, rinsed and patted dry
2 eggs, beaten
1 cup Italian bread crumbs
½ cup finely chopped cooked mushrooms (if using
canned mushrooms, use one 7-oz. can)
1 large onion, thinly sliced
(this will be used for flavoring only)
lemon juice
olive oil
4 sheets of 12" x 16" aluminum foil

Preheat oven to 350° F. In a small mixing bowl, combine bread crumbs, egg and mushrooms. Mix by hand until well blended. Set aside.

On each piece of aluminum foil, lightly spray with olive oil. Brush each cod filet lightly with lemon juice.

Place each fish filet in center of foil. Top each filet with an even layer of stuffing. Brush with lemon juice and olive oil. Cover with onion slices.

Loosely seal packets. Cook at 350° F about 30 minutes until packets puff, or until fish filet meat flakes off with a fork. Open packets and remove onion slices - discard onions! Serve in opened packets. Serves 4.

Tuna with Mango Salsa

2 tuna filets, about ¾ to 1" thick,
fresh, or frozen and thawed
olive oil
salt and cumin

Mango Salsa:
1 cup mango pieces
⅓ cup canned mandarin oranges
⅛ teaspoon onion powder
¼ cup skinless, seedless diced tomatoes

Combine salsa ingredients in a medium mixing bowl. Fold lightly. Set aside.

Lightly brush tuna with olive oil, then sprinkle lightly with salt and cumin. Bake 10 minutes at 400° F or until flaky. Top with salsa.

Salmon Sandwich Rolls

one recipe smoked salmon pâté
4 flour tortillas
1 cup shredded lettuce

On each tortilla, thinly spread ¼ of salmon, then sprinkle evenly with lettuce. Roll, then slice into ½-inch slices, if desired. Serves 4.

Crab Cakes

one 6-oz. can of crab meat, drained
(crab is a caution seafood – try sparingly)
1 egg
¼ cup milk
(see pp 13-14 about lactose)
½ cup Italian bread crumbs

Lightly coat a shallow baking pan with olive oil.
Preheat oven to 350˚ F.

Blend ingredients with a fork. Form into 2- 2 ½ inch
patties, ½ inch thick. Place on pan and bake at 350˚
F for 15 minutes. Makes about 10 crab cakes.

Tuna in Garlic Sauce

two 4-oz. tuna steaks
2 tablespoons olive oil
one recipe Garlic Sauce

Lightly salt and pepper tuna. Lightly brush with
olive oil. Grill over a medium-high flame to desired
doneness, or until flaky (cooking completely through
is considered much safer than any less degree of
doneness).

 Serve with garlic sauce. Serves 2.

Chicken Broth

1½ quarts water
1 pound skinless, boneless chicken
1 teaspoon salt
2 pinches saffron threads

Combine ingredients in a saucepan. Heat to boiling, reduce heat to a gentle boil, cooking until chicken is tender, about 45 minutes. Drain broth through a fine mesh strainer. Reserve chicken for other recipes, such as chicken noodle soup, etc.

Chill broth, then remove any fat from surface before using. Makes about 1 quart.

Chicken Noodle Soup

1 recipe chicken broth,
plus chicken used to make the broth
4 ounces noodles
1 cup carrots, peeled, sliced and cooked until soft

Chop chicken into small chunks. Combine with broth in a saucepan. Heat to boiling.

Add noodles, and cook to according to package instructions. Add carrots one minute before noodles are done cooking. Serves 4.

Vegetable Broth

2 quarts water
4 stalks celery
1 onion
one 6-oz. can of tomato paste
1 teaspoon salt
3 garlic cloves

Boil 30 minutes, or until carrots are soft. Run through strainer. Discard all but broth. Makes about 2 quarts.

Vegetable Noodle Soup

1 quart vegetable broth
2 ounces noodles
1 cup chopped or sliced carrots, cooked until soft
1 cup chopped cooked potatoes

In a large saucepan, bring broth to a boil. Add noodles and cook to package specifications.

One minute before noodles are finished cooking, add potatoes and carrots. Serves 4.

Matzoh Ball Soup

vegetable broth made without tomatoes,
or chicken broth

Matzoh Balls:
¾ cup matzoh meal
4 eggs, 2 yolks removed
3 tablespoons margarine, softened
3 tablespoons water
½ teaspoon salt

Combine matzoh ball ingredients in a mixing bowl. Stir with fork until well blended. Set aside, chilling in refrigerator for at least 30 minutes (chilling overnight is better; the balls will come out feathery.).

Bring 3 quarts of water to boil. While water is heating, remove matzoh dough from fridge. Wet hands with water.

Form dough into one inch balls. Once water has come to a boil, reduce to simmer. Drop balls into gently boiling water. Cover and simmer for about 30 minutes or until cooked throughout.

While matzoh balls are cooking, heat broth on low; this will give it a chance to warm up while preparing matzoh balls.

Remove balls from water with slotted spoon; add to heated broth. Simmer for 5-10 minutes. Serves 4.

French Onion Soup

4 cups water
1 medium to large onion, coarsely chopped
(for flavor only – the onion will be removed)
1 teaspoon salt
1 teaspoon white flour
1 tablespoon canola oil
4 thick slices of French bread
4 slices provolone cheese
(watch for lactose intolerance)

In a non-stick large saucepan, cook onion in canola oil until browned. Sprinkle in flour and continue to cook until browned, stirring constantly.

Quickly add in water, not allowing onions to burn. Add salt.

Bring to a boil. Reduce heat and simmer 20 minutes. Strain and discard onions.

Pour broth into 4 soup bowls. Top with each with a slice of French bread and cheese.

Place in microwave to melt cheese, about 30 seconds each. Serves 4.

Miso Soup

2 cups water
4 teaspoons miso paste
½ cup tofu cut into ½" cubes
2 mushrooms, sliced paper thin

Place water into a saucepan. Bring to a boil. Reduce heat, add miso paste and tofu. Stir gently until miso paste has dissolved. Separate into 2 serving bowls. Add ½ of sliced mushrooms to each immediately before serving. Serves 2.

Potato Soup

2 med-large potatoes, chopped into bite-sized pieces
1 quart water
1 cup skim milk
(see pp 13-14 about lactose)
4 tablespoons flour
1 teaspoon salt
½ teaspoon onion powder

Blend milk, flour, salt and onion powder. Set aside. Boil potatoes in water for 20 minutes, or until tender.

Add milk mixture. Bring to a boil, stirring occasionally. Reduce heat and simmer until desired consistency is reached. Serves 4.

Pumpkin Soup

One 15-oz. can of pumpkin,
or 2 cups cooked, mashed pumpkin
4 cups vegetable or chicken broth
1 teaspoon onion powder
1 cup skim milk
(see pp 13-14 about lactose)
2 tablespoons white flour

Combine all ingredients in a large saucepan. Heat to boiling, stirring frequently with whisk.

Reduce heat and simmer for 2 minutes, stirring frequently. Serves 4-6.

.

Tomato Soup

1 cups tomato juice
1 cups vegetable broth

Combine tomato juice and broth in saucepan. Heat, stirring occasionally. Serves 2.

Fish Salad

two 3-4 ounce filets of mild fish, such as cod
or tilapia, steamed and chilled
4 tablespoons mayonnaise

Blend well in a small mixing bowl. Great for sandwiches and spreads. Makes 4 servings.

Variation: Add 1 chopped boiled egg and ¼ cup steamed, chopped (then chilled) carrots

Chicken and Pasta Salad

¾ lb. chicken, boiled, drained and chopped
2 eggs, boiled, one yolk removed
8 oz. pasta twists
¼ cup mayonnaise

Cook pasta according to package directions. Drain and rinse with cold water until cooled. Place in mixing bowl. Chop eggs and add to pasta.

Add chicken and mayonnaise. Stir well until all is evenly distributed. Makes 5-6 cups.

Chicken Salad

2 cups of cooked, chopped chicken
½ cup mayonnaise
2 boiled eggs, one yolk discarded
¼ teaspoon salt
½ teaspoon onion powder

Boil chicken breast in water until cooked completely through. Drain. Allow chicken to cool. Chop well and place in a medium mixing bowl.

Chop eggs and add to bowl. Add remaining ingredients, mix well until all is evenly distributed. Serves 4.

Egg and Macaroni Salad

½ pound macaroni
⅓ cup mayonnaise
1 boiled egg, coarsely chopped
½ teaspoon garlic powder
½ teaspoon onion powder

Prepare macaroni according to package instructions. Drain well and rinse with cold water.

Toss in remaining ingredients. Chill. Serves 4.

Mushroom Salad

1 pound small whole mushrooms
2 tablespoons olive oil plus ⅔ cup
⅓ cup apple cider vinegar
1 cup canned, diced tomatoes (or fresh - peeled, seeds removed and diced)
1 cup chopped black olives
1 cup feta cheese
(see pp 13-14 about lactose)

Cook mushrooms with 2 tablespoons olive oil in a covered, nonstick pan, about 10 minutes or until cooked; allow to cool.

Combine with remaining ingredients.   Toss and serve. Serves 6.

Potato Salad

3 potatoes, peeled, diced, boiled and chilled, or two 15-oz. cans diced potatoes
3 boiled eggs, 2 yolks discarded, chopped
⅓ cup mayonnaise
½ teaspoon onion powder
½ teaspoon mustard
½ teaspoon salt

Blend all ingredients except potatoes, then fold in potatoes. Chill and serve. Serves 6-8.

Sweet Carrot Salad

2 cups cooked, sliced carrots
One recipe sweet lemon dressing

Gently fold dressing into carrots. Serve heated or
chilled. Makes 2 cups.

Melon Salad

1 medium seedless watermelon half
1 cantaloupe
1 honeydew melon

Hollow out meat from watermelon half and cut into
bite sized pieces or into balls with a melon baller.
Place pieces (or balls) into a large mixing bowl.

Peel and remove ALL seeds from cantaloupe and
melon.   Cut into bite-sized pieces (or balls with
melon baller) and add to bowl. Gently fold until all
is well distributed.

Spoon into hollowed watermelon half and serve, or
cover with plastic wrap and refrigerate.

Any mixture that will not fit into the watermelon
"bowl" can be refrigerated and used for refills.
Serves 6-8.

Fruit Salad

1 ripe cantaloupe
½ cup watermelon pieces, cut with melon baller and
ALL seeds removed
½ cup ripe seedless grapes, peeled

Cut cantaloupe in half. Remove and discard seeds. Hollow out pulp from each half with melon baller.

Place along with remaining ingredients into salad bowl. Fold gently and serve. Serves 4-6.

Broiled Tofu

12 pieces extra firm tofu (½" x 1" x 2")
one recipe sweet lemon dressing

Marinate tofu in dressing for 15 minutes. Lightly mist a cookie sheet with canola oil. Place tofu blocks onto cookie sheet. Do not discard marinade.

Broil at 400° F 4-6 minutes per side, or until lightly browned. Serve drizzled with marinade. Makes one dozen.

Dumplings

1 egg, well beaten
¼ teaspoon salt
½ cup water
2 cups white flour

Combine egg, salt and water. Blend well with a fork. Gradually stir in flour.

Knead lightly with floured hands until dough forms to a ball. Cover and chill for 20 minutes.

Drop dumplings by ½ teaspoonful into boiling water or broth. Cook until done, about 3 minutes.

Serve as part of soup, or separately, topped with sauce, such as Alfredo sauce. Makes about 4 dozen.

Variation: Roll on floured surface to ¼ inch with floured rolling pin. Cut into 1" squares before dropping into boiling water or broth.

Mushrooms in Olive Oil

1 lb. mushrooms
⅛ cup water
2 tablespoons olive oil

Wash mushrooms thoroughly. Slice, or leave whole, if preferred. Combine ingredients in a medium non-stick saucepan. Cooked covered 15 minutes, over medium heat. Uncover and cook, stirring occasionally, until water is reduced. Serve. Makes about 2 cups.

Creamed Spinach

one 10 ounce package frozen, chopped spinach, thawed
¾ cup skim milk
(see pp 13-14 about lactose)
2 teaspoons white flour
½ teaspoon onion powder

Re-chop spinach. Steam spinach, or boil in water, until thoroughly cooked and very soft. Drain.

Combine with remaining ingredients in a medium saucepan. Stir over medium-high heat. Bring to a boil, reduce heat and cook until thickened. Serves 2.

Spinach Risotto

1 cup white rice
2½ cups water
2 tablespoons olive oil
½ teaspoon garlic
½ pound fresh spinach leaves
½ teaspoon salt
¼ cup skim milk
(see pp 13-14 about lactose)

Combine all ingredients, except milk, in large nonstick skillet (preferred thermalon coating). Bring to a boil.

Cover, reduce heat and cook 25 minutes or until rice is cooked.

Uncover, add milk and cook, stirring constantly, until consistency thickens, and risotto is no longer soupy. Serves 4-6.

Stuffed Acorn Squash

one recipe cooked apples
2 acorn squash
2 teaspoons sugar (optional)

Cut squash into halves and remove seeds. Fill with cooked apples. Brush top surface of squash lightly with canola oil. Sprinkle ½ teaspoon sugar over each(optional).

Wrap loosely with aluminum foil. Bake in a 400 degree oven for 1¼ hours, or until squash is tender when pearced with a fork. Serves 4.

Variation: scoop apples and cooked squash from skins, blend with ½ cup brown sugar and serve.

Olive Oil Dip

¼ cup olive oil
2 tablespoons parmesan cheese
½ teaspoon garlic powder

Blend well. Serve in a shallow dish for dipping bread.

Pumpkin Soufflé

one 15-ounce can pumpkin,
or 2 cups cooked, mashed pumpkin
2 eggs, one yolk discarded
¼ teaspoon nutmeg
1 teaspoon cinnamon
¼ teaspoon allspice
⅛ teaspoon cloves
1 cup brown sugar

Lightly coat one 8 x 8 x 2 cooking dish with canola oil. Set aside. Preheat oven to 350° F.

With an electric mixer, blend egg whites until stiff. Set aside.

Combine remaining ingredients in a medium mixing bowl. Blend until smooth..

Add egg white mixture, blending again lightly, but will distributed.

Bake at 350° F for 30 minutes. Serves 4 to 6.

Buttermilk Biscuits

2 cups white flour
½ teaspoon baking soda
¼ teaspoon salt
4 tablespoons margarine, or butter, softened
¾ cup low-fat buttermilk
(see pp 13-14 about lactose)

Preheat oven to 400° F. Lightly mist a cookie sheet with canola oil.

Combine flour, baking soda and salt in a large mixing bowl.

Stir with a for for about 30 seconds, until all ingredients are evenly distributed. Set aside.

Combine margarine with buttermilk, stirring well. Add to flour mixture gradually, stirring first with a ford, then kneading with floured hands.

Place dough on a lightly floured surface. Pat with damp hands to about ½ inch thickness.

Cut in to 3" rounds, then place on cookie sheet.

For best results, brush with buttermilk.

Bake at 400°F for about 15 minutes, or until lightly browned. Makes 9 biscuits.

Carrot Bread

1½ cups minced carrots
2 cups white flour
1 teaspoon salt
2 teaspoons baking powder
⅓ cup brown sugar
1 egg
1 cup skim milk
(see pp 13-14 about lactose)

Preheat oven to 350° F. Lightly coat a 9" x 4" breadpan with canola oil. Set aside.

Combine ingredients in a large mixing bowl. Blend well with an electric mixer.

Transfer to bread pan.

Bake at 350° F for 30 minutes or until a toothpick inserted in the center comes out clean. Allow to cool. Serves 6-8.

Cooked Sweet Potatoes

2 large sweet potatoes
¼ teaspoon cinnamon
¼ teaspoon nutmeg
¼ cup brown sugar
¼ cup skim milk
(see pp 13-14 about lactose)

Peel and chop sweet potatoes. Boil until very soft, about 20 minutes. Blend until smooth with an electric mixer. Sprinkle in cinnamon and nutmeg. Add milk and sugar. Blend again until all is evenly distributed and smooth. Serves 4-6.

Carrots in Herb Sauce

2 cups sliced, peeled carrots (about ½ lb)
1 cup skim milk
(see pp 13-14 about lactose)
¼ teaspoon salt
¼ teaspoon onion powder
¼ teaspoon garlic powder
1 tablespoon white flour
1 teaspoon powdered Italian seasoning

Steam carrots 25 minutes, or until very soft. While carrots are steaming, blend remaining ingredients in a saucepan, bring to a boil, reduce heat and simmer one minute, stirring often. Strain through a fine mesh strainer. Serve over carrots. Serves 4.

Alfredo Sauce

2 cups skim milk
(see pp 13-14 about lactose)
2 tablespoons white flour
½ teaspoon garlic powder
½ teaspoon onion powder
1 teaspoon parsley flakes
½ teaspoon oregano
2 sprinkles pepper
½ teaspoon salt

Combine milk and flour in a mixing bowl. Stir with a fork until the flour is dissolved. Pour into a sauce pan. Place parsley and oregano in a tea ball. Add tea ball and remaining ingredients to saucepan.

Heat to boiling, stirring constantly. Reduce heat and cook for 1-2 minutes, stirring constantly, to desired thickness. Remove tea ball. Serve over pasta or vegetables.

Italian Dressing

¼ cup apple cider vinegar
¾ cup olive or canola oil
½ teaspoon powdered Italian seasoning

Place in a cruet or mason jar, shake well and serve.

Cheese Sauce

1 cup skim milk
2 tablespoons white flour
¼ teaspoon salt
⅔ cup grated Swiss or cheddar cheese
(see pp 13-14 about lactose)

Combine milk, flour and salt in a bowl. Blend with whisk until smooth. Cook to boiling in medium saucepan, then reduce heat to simmer. Add cheese and stir until melted.

Continue to simmer, stirring constantly, for about one minute. Allow to cool for 5 minutes, blend once more with whisk, and serve. Makes about 1 cup.

Garlic Sauce

1 cup skim milk
(see pp 13-14 about lactose)
1 tablespoon white flour
½ teaspoon garlic powder
¼ teaspoon salt

Bring to a boil. Reduce heat and simmer one minute, stirring frequently. Serve. Makes about 1 cup.

Mushroom Sauce

1 cup skim milk
(see pp 13-14 about lactose)
2 tablespoons white flour
one 7-oz. can chopped or sliced mushrooms,
or ½ lb. fresh mushrooms, sliced and cooked

Combine milk with flour. Blend until smooth. Add mushrooms. Cook in a saucepan to boiling, stirring often. Reduce heat and cook one minute, stirring constantly. Serve over meat, bread, potatoes, etc. Makes about 1½ cups.

Blue Cheese Dressing

1 cup fat free plain yogurt
2 oz. fat free cream cheese
½ tablespoon lemon juice
1 cup crumbled blue cheese
(see pp 13-14 about lactose)

Blend cream cheese with an electric mixer until smooth. Add yogurt and lemon juice to cream cheese. Mix again until thoroughly blended. Add in bleu cheese, blend lightly until evenly distributed and serve.

Buttermilk Dressing

¾ cup low fat buttermilk
(see pp 13-14 about lactose)
1 teaspoon brown sugar
1¼ teaspoons lemon juice

Combine ingredients in a quart mason jar. Cover and shake well. Serve immediately over salad.

Sweet Lemon Dressing

2 tablespoons brown sugar
2 tablespoons lemon juice
6 tablespoons canola oil

Combine ingredients in small mixing bowl. Stir until sugar is dissolved. Makes about ⅔ cup.

Spinach Dip

one 8-oz. package cream cheese
¼ teaspoon onion powder
⅛ teaspoon garlic powder
1 lb. spinach, cooked until soft, finely chopped,
drained and patted dry
½ cup sour cream
¼ teaspoon salt
(see pp 13-14 about lactose)

Combine ingredients in a mixing bowl. Blend with an electric mixer until all is well distributed. Makes about 2 cups.

Avocado Spread

2 ripe avocados
1 tablespoon lemon juice
¼ teaspoon powdered garlic
1½ teaspoons cilantro paste
1 tablespoon egg white powder

Remove meat from avocados, mash with fork, add lemon juice and blend thoroughly, blend in remaining ingredients; blend well.

Serve over smoked salmon or white crackers. Makes ¾ to 1 cup.

Baked Butternut Squash

1 butternut squash
2 small onions
2 cloves garlic
olive oil

Cut butternut squash in half. Scoop out seeds. Brush each "bowl" with olive oil. Set aside. Peel and quarter onions and garlic cloves.

Place the quarters of one onion and one garlic clove in each squash "bowl."

Wrap each half loosely with aluminum foil, sealing completely, but allowing room for extra at the top.

Bake at 400° F for 2 to 2½ hours, or until squash is like butter when pierced with a fork.

Discard onion and garlic. Slice each half lengthwise to serve. Serves 4.

Baked Spinach

10 ounce package frozen, chopped spinach, thawed
¾ cup skim milk
(see pp 13-14 about lactose)
⅛ cup white flour
½ teaspoon onion powder
½ teaspoon salt
2 eggs

Preheat oven to 350° F. Lightly coat 8 x 8 x 2 baking dish with canola oil. Set aside.

Drain and re-chop spinach. Combine with remaining ingredients in a mixing bowl.

Blend well with electric mixer. Transfer to casserole dish. Bake at 350° F for 30 minutes. Serves 4.

Cream Cheese Florentine

one 8-oz. package cream cheese
(see pp 13-14 about lactose)
⅛ teaspoon onion powder
⅛ teaspoon garlic powder
2 oz. frozen spinach, cooked until soft, finely chopped, drained and patted dry

Blend with mixer. Makes about 1¼ cups.

Cooked Apples

2 apples
⅓ cup water
2½ tablespoons sugar
One 1" chunk of ginger root, peeled and quartered
1 tablespoon lemon juice
½ teaspoon vanilla extract

Peel, core and finely slice apples. Set aside. Combine water and sugar, stirring until sugar is dissolved. Place into medium non-stick saucepan.

Add remaining ingredients, including apple slices. Cook over medium high heat, stirring occasionally, for about 10 minutes or until apples have softened. Remove ginger. Continue cooking until liquid is reduced and apples are slightly browned. Serve warm. Serves 2-4.

Cherry Sauce

⅔ cup water
⅓ cup sugar
2 tablespoons white flour
1 tablespoon tart cherry juice concentrate

Blend ingredients with a whisk. Bring to boil in a medium saucepan. Reduce heat and simmer one minutes stirring constantly. Serve over yogurt, ice cream or cake.

Cherry Mousse

One 3-oz. box of cherry flavored Jello
2 egg whites
1 tablespoon tart cherry juice concentrate
½ cup powdered sugar

Prepare Jello according to package directions. Once Jello has chilled for 1¼ hours, prepare egg white mixture: Place two egg whites in mixing bowl. Blend with electric mixer until stiff. Add cherry concentrate and sugar. Blend well. Add to jello mixture, blending well. Transfer to dessert dishes. Chill an additional 3 hours. Serves 4-6.

Rice Pudding

1½ cups cooked rice
½ cup brown sugar, packed
1 egg
½ teaspoon cinnamon

Preheat oven at 350° F. Lightly coat a 9 x 5 x 3 bread pan with canola oil. Combine ingredients in a mixing bowl. Stir with spoon until evenly distributed. The brown sugar and egg will blend together to form a sort of syrup. Pack mixture firmly in bread pan. Cook at 350° F for 40 minutes. Remove from oven, cool 10 minutes, fluff with fork and serve. Serves 4.

Carrot Cake

Cake:

1½ cups minced carrots
2 cups white flour
1 teaspoon salt
2 teaspoons baking powder
1 cup brown sugar
1 egg
1 cup skim milk
(see pp 13-14 about lactose)

Cream Cheese Icing:

⅔ cup cream cheese
(see pp 13-14 about lactose)
1 cup powdered sugar

Cake: Preheat oven to 350° F. Lightly coat 8 x 8 x 2 cooking pan with canola oil. Set aside.

Combine ingredients in a large mixing bowl. Blend well with an electric mixer. Transfer to bread pan.

Bake at 350° F for 45-50 minutes or until a toothpick inserted in the center comes out clean. Cool completely, top with icing and serve.

Icing: While cake is cooling, combine ingredients in a small mixing bowl. Blend with an electric mixer until smooth. Serves 4-6.

Lemon Pudding

3 tablespoons white flour
½ cup sugar
2 cups skim milk
(see pp 13-14 about lactose)
2 eggs, one yolk discarded
1 teaspoon vanilla extract
¼ cup lemon juice

Blend all ingredients except lemon juice with a whisk until smooth.

Cook in a non-stick saucepan over medium to high heat, stirring frequently, until mixture begins to thicken, about 20 minutes.

Add lemon juice and cook, stirring constantly, one minute.

Remove from heat, pour into serving dishes and allow to cool.

Pudding will thicken more as it cools. Serve chilled. Serves 4.

Peaches and Cream

2 large peaches, peeled and sliced
¾ cup skim milk
(see pp 13-14 about lactose)
1 tablespoon white flour
¼ teaspoon vanilla extract
⅛ cup sugar
nutmeg

Steam peaches for 15 minutes, or until soft enough to cut with a fork. While peaches are steaming, prepare sauce:

Combine milk, flour, vanilla and sugar in a small saucepan. Bring to a boil, then reduce heat to medium.

Cook, stirring constantly with a whisk, for about 10 minutes. Sauce will cook down to about ½ cup. Remove from heat.

Divide peaches into 4 serving bowls. Pour sauce on top and sprinkle very lightly with nutmeg.
3 ½ cups. Serves 4.

Phase Three Recipes

Apple Cherry Tea

2 cups water
2 cups apple juice
2 tablespoons tart cherry juice concentrate
1 cinnamon sticks
4 whole cloves

Combine ingredients in saucepan and bring to a boil. Reduce heat and simmer for 10 minutes. Remove cinnamon and cloves. Serve warm. Makes one quart.

Cherry Shake

3 tablespoons tart cherry juice concentrate
2 cups milk
¼ cup sugar
½ cup plain nonfat yogurt
(see pp 13-14 about lactose)

Combine in blender and mix until smooth. Makes about 3 cups.

Paella

1 cup white rice
2 cups water
2 pinches saffron threads
one 8-oz. can of oysters
one 4.25-oz. can of lump crab meat
one 6.5 oz. can of minced clams
½ teaspoon powdered garlic
½ teaspoon powdered onion
½ teaspoon salt

Bring ingredients to boil in a large non-stick skillet, recommend thermalon coating. Stir weel, cover and reduce heat.

Simmer 20 minutes or until water is absorbed. Remove from heat and allow to sit for 5 minutes before serving. Serves 4-6.

Warm Potato Salad

3 potatoes, peeled, diced and boiled
⅓ cup apple cider vinegar
⅔ cup canola oil
½ cup chopped boiled ham

Toss and serve. Serves 4-6.

Chicken and Dumplings

1½ quarts water
1 pound chicken breast, cut into bite-sized chunks
2 cups skim milk
(see pp 13-14 about lactose)
8 tablespoons white flour
1½ teaspoons salt
one recipe dumpling dough (page 64)

Bring ½ quart of water to a boil. Drop in chicken breast, boil until chicken is cooked. Drain.

While chicken is boiling, prepare dumpling dough.

Combine remaining water, chicken and salt in a large cooking pot.

Bring to a boil, stirring occasionally. Add dumpling dough ½ teaspoon at a time, cooking until dumplings are done, about 3 minutes.

In a small mixing bowl, combine milk and flour. Blend well. Add to pot.

Continue cooking, stirring often. Cook to desired consistency. Serves 4.

Baked Stuffed Flounder

4 flounder filets
1 - 6 oz. can of crab meat, drained
(crab is a caution seafood – try sparingly)
1 egg (pre-pasteurized)
¼ cup milk
(see pp 13-14 about lactose)
2 tablespoons olive oil
1 teaspoon lemon juice

Lightly coat 8 x 8 x 2 baking dish with olive oil. Set aside. Preheat oven to 350° F.

Rinse flounder filets with water. Pat dry. Set aside. Combine crab meat, milk, egg and bread crumbs in a small mixing bowl. Blend with a fork. Set aside.

Blend olive oil and lemon juice in a small mixing bowl. Lay flounder on a flat surface. Brush both sides with olive oil mixture.

Spread one fourth of crabmeat mixture evenly over each filet. Roll and place into cooking dish, seam side down. Fix with toothpick if needed.

Bake at 350° F for 15 minutes, or until fish flakes away with a fork. Serves 4.

Pot Roast

one 2-3 pound pot roast
one onion, quartered
2 potatoes, peeled and cut into chunks
4 carrots, peeled and cut into bite size pieces
4 cloves garlic
2 teaspoons salt
4 cups water

Place ingredients, in slow cooker. Cook on low setting for 8-9 hours or until meat is tender. Serve meat and vegetables with a slotted spoon, discarding onion and garlic. Top with strained stock from slow cooker.

French Dip

leftover pot roast (see recipe above), chilled
once recipe au jus sauce (page 90)
provolone cheese*, thinly sliced
(optional - (see pp 13-14 about lactose)
French baguettes

Slice pot roast as thinly as possible. Place au jus and pot roast slices in saucepan to warm. For each French dip serving, cut baguette in half, place one layer of pot roast and top with sliced provolone.

To eat, dip in warmed au jus prior to each bite.

Ginger Beef

1 to 1½ pounds lean stew meat,
cut into bite size pieces
2 chunks (about 1" cubes) of ginger root, peeled
½ teaspoon garlic powder
½ teaspoon salt
2 quarts water
one large onion , quartered
one recipe ginger sauce (below)

Combine all ingredients, except ginger sauce, in a slow cooker. Cook 8-9 hours on low setting, or 5-6 on high, until meat is tender. Prepare ginger sauce; set aside. Drain meat, discarding liquid, onions and ginger. Serve meat topped with ginger sauce.

Ginger Sauce

1 cup water
⅜ cup brown sugar, packed
3 tablespoons lemon juice
2 tablespoons white flour
½ teaspoon onion powder
¼ teaspoon garlic powder
¼ cup soy sauce, reduced sodium

Combine in mixing bowl. Blend with whisk until all is dissolved. Heat in saucepan to boiling, reduce heat and simmer one minute, stirring constantly. Serve over meat, fish or vegetables. Makes about 1½ cups.

Au Jus Sauce

one Pot Roast recipe (page 88)

Prepare pot roast recipe according to directions. Strain through a fine mesh strainer, reserving juice.

Chill juice for at least one hour, or long enough for fat to separate to the top.

Remove fat carefully with a spoon, by gently submerging the spoon just enough for the separated fat to flow into it.

Discard fat. Continue by spoonfuls until all has been removed.

OR (preferred method:), if time allows, chill long enough for fat to solidify at top for easier removal.

Warm before serving. Makes about 3cups.

Shepherd's Pie

1 pound meat from pot roast recipe (page 88)
2 cups chilled broth from pot roast recipe (fat removed)
1 cup of cooked, sliced carrots
4 tablespoons white flour
2 medium potatoes, peeled and chopped
½ cup milk
(see pp 13-14 about lactose)
½ teaspoon salt

Preheat oven to 350° F.

Cook potatoes by boiling or steaming until very soft. Drain. Mash with potato masher, add milk and salt, mashing again until creamy. Set aside.

Combine broth with flour in a small mixing bowl. Blend with a fork or whisk until smooth. Pour into a medium saucepan, adding meat and carrots.

Bring to a boil, stirring often. Reduce heat and simmer until the sauce thickens.

Transfer into a 2-quart casserole dish or an 8 x 8 x 2 cooking dish.

Place mashed potatoes on top, gently spreading evenly across. Bake for 30 minutes at 350° F. Serves 4-6.

Mock Stroganoff

½ pound egg noodles
½ pound lean ground beef
1 cup skim milk*
2 tablespoons white flour
½ teaspoon onion powder
½ teaspoon garlic powder
1 teaspoon salt
½ cup sour cream*

In a small mixing bowl, combine milk, flour, onion powder, garlic powder and salt. Blend until smooth. Set aside.

Prepare noodles according to package instructions. While noodles are cooking:

Make miniature patties with hamburger, about 1 inch in diameter and ¼ inch thickness.

Cook patties in a large, nonstick skillet. Drain fat. Add milk mixture. Bring to a boil, gently stirring. Reduce heat and cook 1-2 minutes, or until sauce is thick.

Stir in sour cream. Serve over noodles. Serves 4.

*see pp 13-14 about lactose intolerance. The milk can be substituted with Lactaid, soy milk or almond milk. The sour cream can be substituted with ½ cup Lactaid cottage cheese plus 1½ teaspoons lemon juice pureed in a blender until smooth.

Meatballs in Mushroom Sauce

½ pound lean ground beef
¾ cup finely ground Italian bread crumbs
½ cup milk
(see pp 13-14 about lactose)
½ teaspoon salt
2 eggs
one recipe mushroom sauce (page 74)

Lightly coat a cooking pan with canola oil. Preheat oven to 350° F.

Combine all ingredients except mushroom sauce, mixing by hand until smooth. Divide into 12 equal portions.

Shape into balls and place in cooking pan. Bake 30 minutes at 350° F.

Top with one recipe mushroom sauce. Makes one dozen. Serves 4-6.

Meatloaf

1 pound lean ground beef
1 egg
¼ cup skim milk
(see pp 13-14 about lactose)
½ cup white flour
1 teaspoon onion powder
1 teaspoon garlic powder
1 teaspoon salt

Preheat oven to 350˚ F. Lightly coat a small loaf pan with canola oil. Set aside.

Combine ingredients in a medium mixing bowl.

Knead by hand until all is evenly distributed and mixture gains a smooth texture. Place in bread pan.

Cook at 350˚ F for 45-50 minutes or until internal temperature reaches 170˚ F.

Serve in one-inch slices topped with mushroom or white onion sauce.

Meatloaf Patties

½ pound lean ground beef
1 cup cooked rice
2 eggs
1 quart smooth tomato sauce
¼ cup white flour
½ teaspoon salt

Lightly coat a large cooking pan with olive oil. Preheat oven to 350° F. Blend all ingredients except 3 cups sauce. Mix by hand until all is evenly blended.

Texture will be almost soupy. With wet hands, roll into 3" patties. Bake at 350° F for 30-35 minutes or until nicely browned.

While patties are cooking, heat remainder of sauce in a saucepan over low heat. Serve meatballs topped with sauce. Makes about one dozen.

Lasagna

1½ cups fat free ricotta or cottage cheese
2 quarts smooth tomato sauce
1 pound lean ground beef
1 package lasagna noodles
½ pound reduced fat mozzarella cheese, grated
(see pp 13-14 about lactose)

Preheat oven to 350° F.

Prepare noodles according to package directions. Drain, rinse and set aside.

While noodles are cooking, brown the beef in a skillet, drain and place in mixing bowl with spaghetti sauce. Add ricotta. Stir until evenly distributed. Set aside. Lightly coat a deep 10 x 15 baking dish with olive oil. Place one layer of lasagna noodles, side by side, in the bottom of the dish.

Spread an even layer of sauce over the noodles. Over the sauce, place a layer of ¼ of the mozzarella. Proceed with additional layers of noodles, sauce and mozzarella, ending on the top with a layer of noodles.

Cover the noodles completely with a final layer of sauce. This will keep the noodles from drying out in the oven. Bake at 350° F for about 45 minutes, or until sauce on top begins to brown. Allow to cool at least 10 minutes before serving. Makes 12-15 servings.

Peasant Cheese Casserole

4 slices of cubed French bread (slightly stale is OK)
1½ cups gruyere cheese, grated
4 eggs
1½ cups skim milk
(see pp 13-14 about lactose)
1½ teaspoons smooth brown mustard
1 teaspoon salt

Preheat oven to 350° F. Lightly coat a 2 quart casserole dish with canola oil.

Place bread in casserole dish. Top with cheese. Set aside.

Combine remaining ingredients in a medium mixing bowl. Blend with a whisk until smooth. Pour gently over ingredients in casserole dish.

Lightly press down any bread that is not covered by the milk mixture.

Bake at 350° F for 45 minutes. Allow to cool 10 minutes before serving. Serve hot or warm. Serves 4-6.

Ham Salad

½ lb. ham, boiled, drained and chilled
¼ cup mayo
4 oz. cooked pasta

Dice ham. Fold in pasta and mayo. Serve chilled. Makes about 3 cups.

Clam Chowder

1 can minced clams*
2 med-large potatoes, chopped into bite-sized pieces
3cups water
1 cup clam juice
1 cup skim milk
(see pp 13-14 about lactose)
4 tablespoons white flour
1 teaspoon salt
½ teaspoon onion powder

Blend milk, flour, salt and onion powder. Set aside. Combine potatoes, clams, water and clam juice in a large cooking pot. Boil for about 30 minutes, or until clams and potatoes are tender.   Add milk mixture. Bring to a boil, stirring occasionally. Reduce heat and simmer, stirring occasionally, until desired consistency is reached. Serves 4.

*Remember, clams are a "caution" seafood. Try sparingly!

Beef and Barley Stew

2-3 pound pot roast or lean stew meat
4 cups water
2 teaspoons salt
1 teaspoon onion powder
1 teaspoon garlic powder
¾ cup barley
2 cups of peeled, chopped carrots

Cut meat into bite sized chunks, trimming off fat. Place all ingredients in a slow cooker.

Cook 10-11 hours on low, or until meat becomes tender enough to fall apart. Turn off slow cooker.

Strain meat, reserving broth. Place broth in refrigerator or freezer until fat solidifies on top (Meat may be refrigerated as well). Remove fat.

Place broth back into slow cooker with meat. Add carrots and barley.

Cook on high until carrots are very soft, about 2 ½ hours. Serves 6-8.

Cheese Soup

3 cups skim milk
1 teaspoon smooth Dijon mustard
2 tablespoons white flour
4 ounces reduced fat sharp cheddar cheese
½ teaspoon salt
(see pp 13-14 about lactose)

Combine all ingredients except cheese in a saucepan.
Blend with whisk until smooth. Add cheese and stir.

Bring to a boil, then reduce heat and cook, stirring
frequently, until cheese is melted and soup is slightly
thickened, about 20 minutes. Serves 4.

Crab and Macaroni Salad

½ pound macaroni
one 4.25 ounce can crab meat
(crab is a caution seafood – try sparingly!)
⅓ cup mayonnaise
1 cup chopped black olives

Prepare macaroni according to package instructions.
Drain, cover and chill. Toss chilled macaroni with
remaining ingredients. Serve chilled. Makes about 5
cups.

Crabmeat Salad

One 6-oz. can lump crabmeat
(crab is a caution seafood – try sparingly!)
2 tablespoons mayonnaise
1 boiled egg, finely chopped
⅛ teaspoon onion powder
⅛ cup cooked minced carrots

Combine ingredients in a mixing bowl. Blend until all is well distributed. Works well as a salad, spread or dip. Serves 2.

Spinach Sandwich Rolls

4 flour tortillas
4 ounces fat free cream cheese
⅜ cup feta cheese
10 ounces fresh or frozen chopped spinach
(see pp 13-14 about lactose)

Boil or steam spinach until very soft. Drain, chop and pat dry.

In a small mixing bowl, blend cream cheese, feta and spinach with electric mixer. Spread ¼ of mixture evenly on each tortilla. Roll, slice if desired, and serve. Serves 4.

Broccoli in Ginger Sauce

2 heads of broccoli
1 tablespoon white flour
¼ cup brown sugar
one 1-inch chunk of ginger root, peeled
1 clove garlic
1 tablespoon lemon juice
1 cup water

Chop broccoli. Steam broccoli about 20 minutes, or until very soft.

While steaming broccoli, Combine water and flour in a small mixing bowl.

Blend until smooth. Transfer to a sauce pan.

Add remaining ingredients. Bring to a boil while stirring often.

Reduce heat to low and continue cooking, stirring constantly, until desired thickness is reached.

Remove ginger and garlic. Drizzle sauce over cooked broccoli and serve. Serves 4.

Variation: Top broccoli with hollandaise sauce.

Mushroom Risotto

3 tablespoons olive oil
½ lb mushrooms, chopped
1 cup white rice
2½ cups water
¼ teaspoon salt
1 cube onion puree or ½ teaspoon onion powder
½ teaspoon garlic powder
¼ cup skim milk
(see pp 13-14 about lactose)

Combine mushrooms, olive oil and onion puree in sauce pan, covered, over medium heat, about 5 minutes or until mushrooms are cooked.

Add rice, stirring well until rice is well coated with olive oil.

Add remaining ingredients except milk. Stir, bring to a boil, reduce heat, cover and cook 20 minutes, undisturbed.

Remove cover, increase heat to med-high, add milk.

Cook, stirring Constantly, until it reaches a creamy texture(not soupy). Serves 6.

Stuffed Potatoes

4 medium to large potatoes
1 cup grated cheddar cheese
1 egg
¼ cup skim milk
(see pp 13-14 about lactose)
¼ teaspoon salt

Bake potatoes for 1½ hours at 350° F, or until a fork inserts easily, set aside to cool. Combine remaining ingredients in a mixing bowl. Scoop out potatoes, leaving ¼ inch thickness with skins. Add to mixing bowl. Mash, Pipe or spoon into potato skins.

Sprinkle lightly with paprika. Bake 30 minutes at 350° F. The skins are for decoration only. Do not eat! Serves 8.

White Onion Sauce

1 cup skim milk
(see pp 13-14 about lactose)
3 cubes onion puree (page 105),
or 1 teaspoon onion powder
1 tablespoon white flour
½ teaspoon salt

Heat to boiling, stirring often. Reduce heat and cook one minute, stirring constantly.

Serve over noodles, potatoes or vegetables.

Onion Puree

6 cups of coarsely chopped onions
1 cup water
1 ice tray, dedicated to onions

Combine onions and water in saucepan. Cook until onions are transparent and water is reduced. Allow to cool, transfer to blender, puree.

Transfer puree to ice tray. After frozen, remove puree cubes and seal in a zipper bag.

Remove cubes as needed, using for flavor in recipes.

One cube added to represents about ½ cup of chopped onion. Makes about one tray, or 2 cups.

Teriyaki Marinade

1½ cup low sodium soy sauce
1 cup water
⅓ cup apple cider vinegar
¼ cup sugar
½ teaspoon garlic powder
½ teaspoon dried ground ginger

Combine and stir until all is dissolved. Marinade meat (chicken, beef or fish for at least two hours before cooking. Makes about 3 cups.

Mushroom Curry

¼ cup water
1 tablespoon curry powder
½ teaspoon onion powder
1 pound sliced mushrooms
¾ cup skim milk
(see pp 13-14 about lactose)
½ teaspoon salt
1½ tablespoons white flour

Put all but milk and flour in a saucepan. Cook until mushrooms are fully done. Whisk milk and flour together, add to mushrooms, bring to a boil, reduce heat and cook 1 minute, stirring often. Serve over rice or fish.

Tomato Rice

1 cup white rice
⅔ cup water
1⅓ cups tomato juice
1 tomato, skin and seeds removed, chopped,
or one 14-15 oz. can chopped tomatoes
½ teaspoon salt
1 tablespoon canola oil

Combine all ingredients in a medium saucepan. Bring to a boil. Stir and continue to boil for about 30 seconds. Cover and reduce heat to simmer, undisturbed, for 15-20 minutes, or until liquid is absorbed. Remove from heat and leave covered for 5 minutes.

Serve hot, topped with grated Parmesan or Romano cheese. Serves 4.

Spaghetti Squash

1 spaghetti squash
water
2 tablespoons olive oil
grated parmesan cheese
one recipe Alfredo sauce (page 72)

Cut squash in half. Scoop out seeds with a large spoon.

Place spaghetti squash in a Dutch oven baking dish. Brush with olive oil. Place enough water to cover ¼ inch in the bottom of the Dutch oven.

Bake, covered, at 425° F, for 1½ hours, or until a fork inserted into the squash glides in easily.

During the last 20 minutes of baking, prepare the Alfredo sauce. Remove squash from oven. With a fork, gently lift out cooked strands into a serving dish. Top with Alfredo sauce. Serves 4-6.

Stuffed Mushrooms

12 large mushrooms
One 6-oz. can of crabmeat
(crab is a caution seafood – try sparingly!)
1 egg
¼ cup feta cheese, crumbled
(see pp 13-14 about lactose)
¼ cup Italian bread crumbs

Preheat oven to 350° F. Lightly coat a 9x13x2 pan with olive oil. Set aside.

Remove stems from mushrooms.

Chop finely and place in mixing bowl. Add crabmeat, egg, cheese and bread crumbs.

Mix by hand until thoroughly blended.

Fill mushroom caps, place in cooking pan. Spray lightly with olive oil.

Cover and bake at 350° F for 45 minutes. Makes one dozen.

Tomato Cream Sauce

1 cup skim milk
(see pp 13-14 about lactose)
2 tablespoons white flour
3 tablespoons tomato paste
1 teaspoon powdered Italian seasoning
pinch of salt
pinch of pepper

Combine milk with flour, mixing with a whisk until flour is dissolved.

Gradually add salt, pepper and tomato paste to milk mixture, stirring with whisk, until ingredients are well blended.

Transfer to a sauce pan.   Place Italian seasoning in a tea ball and add to saucepan.

Heat to boiling, stirring often. Reduce heat and cook one minute, stirring constantly.

Serve over pasta, vegetables or eggs. Makes about one cup.

Twice Baked Sweet Potatoes

4 medium sized sweet potatoes
½ cup packed brown sugar
½ tsp nutmeg
¼ tsp cloves
¼ tsp allspice
½ tsp cinnamon
1 egg

Preheat oven 350° F. Wrap potatoes in foil. Cook in 350 degree oven for 45 minutes, or until a fork inserted into the middle glides in smoothly.

Allow to cool completely.

Lightly coat a 2 quart casserole dish with canola oil. Set aside.

Remove and discard peels. Place potatoes in a large mixing bowl.

Add remaining ingredients and blend well with an electric mixer.

Place in a casserole dish. Bake at 350° F for 30 minutes. Serve warm or cold. Serves 6-8.

Bread Pudding

2 chopped peeled peaches,
or one 15 oz. can of peaches in peach juice,
drained and chopped
2 cups skim milk
(see pp 13-14 about lactose)
1 teaspoon vanilla
¾ cup sugar
1 pinch ground cloves
⅛ teaspoon cinnamon
⅛ teaspoon nutmeg
4 cups cubed white bread (stale is OK)
1 egg

Preheat oven to 350° F. Lightly coat an 8" x 8" x 2" oven dish with canola oil. Set aside.

Combine all ingredients in a large mixing bowl.

Blend well. Pour into oven dish.

Cook 1¼ hours at 350° F.

Allow to cool at least 15 minutes before serving.

Pumpkin Bread

1 cup pumpkin, either canned, or cooked and pushed
through a fine mesh strainer
1½ cups white flour
1 teaspoon baking soda
½ teaspoon salt
1 recipe pumpkin pie spice (page 113)
1 cup sugar
½ cup sour cream*
1 egg
2 tablespoons canola oil

Lightly coat one 9 x 4 bread pan with canola oil.
Combine ingredients in a large mixing bowl.

Blend with electric mixer until smooth.

Bake in bread pan at 350° F for 45-50 minutes or
until knife inserted in center comes out clean.

Cool at least 10 minutes before serving.

*see pp 13-14 about lactose intolerance. The sour cream can be
substituted with ½ cup Lactaid cottage cheese plus 1½ teaspoons
lemon juice, pureed in a blender until smooth.

Pumpkin Pie Spice

1 teaspoon cinnamon
¼ teaspoon nutmeg
¼ teaspoon ginger
⅛ teaspoon allspice
⅛ teaspoon ground cloves

Combine ingredients in a small mixing bowl. Blend well until all is evenly distributed. Makes 1¾ tsp.

Guacamole

3 ripe avocados
1½ tablespoons lemon juice
¼ cup tomatoes (optional), steamed, peeled, seeded and diced
⅛ teaspoon salt
¼ teaspoon onion powder
¼ teaspoon garlic powder
Cilantro paste or spritz to equal 1 tablespoon fresh cilantro

Half avocadoes. Scoop out meat and place in mixing bowl. Immediately add lemon juice and mash with fork. Sprinkle in remaining ingredients, stirring until well blended. Serve immediately as a side dish or as a dip. Makes 1½ to 2 cups.

Bibliography

Bonci, Leslie, MPH, RD, American Dietetic Association Guide to Better Digestion, 2003, Hoboken, NJ, John Wiley & Sons, Inc.

Dalessandro, Tracie Rendino, MS, RD, CDN, What to Eat with IBD; A Comprehensive Nutrition and Recipe Guide for Crohn's Disease and Ulcerative Colitis, 2006, Briarcliff Manor, NY, CMG Publishing

Duyff, Roberta Larson, MS, RD, FADA, CFCS, *American Dietetic Association Complete Food and Nutrition Guide*, 3rd Edition, 2006, Hoboken, NJ, John Wiley & Sons, Inc., pp. 523-530, 579-582

Finlandia, America's #1 Imported deli cheese, Finlandia Cheese, http://www.finlandiacheese.com/healthy_lactose.html, July 10, 2012

Gibbons, De Lamar, MD, The Self-Help Way to Treat Colitis and Other IBS Conditions, 2nd Edition, 2001, New York, NY, McGraw-Hill

International Foundation for Functional Gastrointestinal Disorders - iffgd.org, International Foundation for Functional Gastrointestinal Disorders (IFFGD) Inc., http://www.iffgd.org, July 18, 2012

Kane, Sunanda V., MD, MSPH, IBD Self Management: The AGA Guide to Crohn's Disease and Ulcerative Colitis, 2010, Bethesda, MD, AGA Press

Lactaid® Brand Health Living with Lactose Intolerance, McNeill Nutritionals, LLC, http://www.lactaid.com/node/3, July 18, 2012

Lactose Intolerance - National Digestive Diseases Information Clearinghouse, National Institute of Diabetes and Digestive and Kidney Diseases, National Institutes of Health, http://digestive.niddk.nih.gov/ddiseases/pubs/lactoseintolerance/#man aged, July 10, 2012

McGee, Harold, Keys to good cooking: a guide to making the best of foods and recipes, 2010, New York, NY, Penguin Press, pp 105-118, 211-236, 187-322

Ramancher, Sandra, Healing Foods; Cooking for Celiacs, Colitis, Crohn's and IBS, 2007, Noosaville, Qld Australia, Elephant Publishing Pty Ltd.

Recipe Converter, McNeill Nutritionals, LLC, http://www.lactaid.com/recipes/recipe-conversion, July 18, 2012

Scala, James, Ph.D., The New Eating Right for a Bad Gut; the complete nutritional guide to ileitis, colitis, Crohn's disease, and inflammatory bowel disease, 1st edition revised, New York, NY, Plume (a member of Penguin Putnam Inc.)

University Health Center | Nutrition | Lactose Intolerance, Division of Student Affairs, University of Georgia, http://www.uhs.uga.edu/nutrition/lactoseintolerance.html, July 10, 2012

Vanaman, Bonnie, Tart Cherry Juice for Arthritis|Livestrong.com, http://www.livestrong.com/article/461479-tart-cherry-juice-for-arthritis/, 8/5/12

Warner, Andrew S, M.D. & Barto, Amy E., M.D., 100 Questions & Answers about Crohn's disease and ulcerative colitis; a Lahey Clinic guide, 2007, Sudbury, MA, Jones and Bartlett Publishers, Inc.

Cod in Pouches, Stuffed, 50
Cooked Apples, 79
Cooked Mushrooms, 42
Cooked Sweet Potatoes, 71
Crab and Macaroni Salad, 100
Crab Cakes, 52
Crabmeat Salad, 101
Cranberry Tea, 31
Cream Cheese Florentine, 78
Cream, Peaches and, 83
Cream Sauce, Tomato, 109
Creamed Rice, 48
Creamed Spinach, 65
Crepes, Apple, 46
Crepes, Cherry Yogurt, 47
Croquettes, Salmon, 49
Curry, Mushroom, 106
Devilled Eggs, 41
Dip, French, 88
Dip, Olive Oil, 67
Dip, Spinach, 76
Dressing, Blue Cheese, 74
Dressing, Buttermilk, 75
Dressing, Italian, 72
Dressing, Sweet Lemon, 75
Dumplings, 64
Dumplings, Chicken and, 86
Egg and Macaroni Salad, 60
Egg Drop Soup, 40
Egg Salad, 40

Egg Sauce, 43
Eggs, Boiled, 34
Eggs, Devilled, 41
Eggs, Poached, 36
Eggs, Scrambled, 34
Fish, Marinated Grilled, 39
Fish Salad, 59
Florentine, Cream Cheese, 78
Flounder, Baked, 38
Flounder, Baked Stuffed, 87
French Onion Soup, 56
French Dip, 88
French Toast, 35
Fruit Salad, 63
Garlic Sauce, 73
Garlic Sauce, Tuna in, 52
Ginger Beef, 89
Ginger Sauce, 89
Ginger Sauce, Broccoli in, 102
Grilled Fish, Marinated, 39
Grouper, Broiled, 37
Guacamole, 113
Ham Salad, 98
Herb Sauce, Carrots in, 71
Homemade Low-fat Yogurt, 38
Italian Dressing, 72
Lasagna, 96
Lemon Dressing, Sweet, 75
Lemon Pudding, 82

Pudding, Lemon, 82
Pudding, Rice, 80
Pudding, Vanilla, 44
Pumpkin Bread, 112
Pumpkin Pie Spice, 113
Pumpkin Soufflé, 68
Pumpkin Soup, 58
Puree, Onion, 105
Rice, Creamed, 48
Rice Pudding, 80
Rice,Tomato, 106
Risotto, Mushroom, 103
Risotto, Spinach, 66
Roast, Pot, 88
Rolls, Salmon Sandwich, 52
Rolls, Spinach Sandwich, 101
Salad, Chicken, 60
Salad, Chicken and Pasta, 59
Salad, Crab and Macaroni, 100
Salad, Crabmeat, 101
Salad, Egg, 40
Salad, Egg and Macaroni, 60
Salad, Fish, 59
Salad, Fruit, 63
Salad, Ham, 98
Salad, Melon, 62
Salad, Mushroom, 61
Salad, Potato, 61
Salad, Sweet Carrot, 62
Salad, Warm Potato, 85

Salmon Croquettes, 49
Salmon Pâté, Smoked, 39
Salmon Sandwich Rolls, 52
Salsa, Tuna with Mango, 51
Sandwich Rolls, Salmon, 52
Sandwich Rolls, Spinach, 101
Sauce, Alfredo, 72
Sauce, Au Jus, 90
Sauce, Broccoli in Ginger, 102
Sauce, Carrots in Herb, 71
Sauce, Cheese, 73
Sauce, Cherry, 79
Sauce, Egg, 43
Sauce, Garlic, 73
Sauce, Ginger, 89
Sauce, Meatballs in
   Mushroom, 93
Sauce, Mushroom, 74
Sauce, Tomato Cream, 109
Sauce, Tuna in Garlic, 52
Sauce, White Onion, 104
Scrambled Eggs, 34
Shake, Cherry, 84
Shake, Mango, 29
Shake, Orange, 30
Shake, Peach, 45
Shake, Vanilla, 30
Shepherd's Pie, 91
Smoked Salmon Pâté, 39
Soufflé, Pumpkin, 68

www.ingramcontent.com/pod-product-compliance
Lightning Source LLC
Chambersburg PA
CBHW060945040426
42445CB00011B/1005